simple
home
❖ style ❖

simple
home
style

TESSA EVELEGH

Photographs by Polly Wreford

Watson-Guptill Publications/New York

Acknowledgments

I would like to thank all the contributors, without whom this book would never have happened:
Caroline Cilia for the Driftwood Bathmat; Karin Hossack for the Mosaic Cabinet, the Studded Coffee Table, and the Felt Placemats; Andrew Gillmore for the Hammered Mirror Frame; Mary Maguire for the Beaded Lampshade; Kerry Skinner for the Metallic-Effect Cabinet, Découpage Chest, and Painted Floorcloth; Isabel Stanley for the Fishy Appliqué Tablecloth; and Sarah Clarke for the curtains and placemats. My special thanks to Polly Wreford for her stunning photography, and to Lucy Pope for creating the step-by-step photographs.

Thanks also to the suppliers: Damask, Broxholme House, New King's Road, London SW6 4AA, for bed and table linens and home accessories; Artisan, Unit 4A Union Court, 20 Union Road, London SW4 6JP, for curtain poles and metal hooks; and Edgar Udny, 314 Balham High Road, London SW17 7AA, for mosaic tiles.

Published by MQ Publications, Ltd.,
254–258 Goswell Road,
London EC1V 7EB
Series Editor: Ljiljana Ortolja-Baird
Designer: Bet Ayer

First published in the United States in 1998
by Watson-Guptill Publications,
a division of BPI Communications, Inc.,
1515 Broadway, New York, N.Y. 10036

Library of Congress Catalog Card Number: 97-62231

ISBN 0-8230-4800-4

Printed in Italy

First printing, 1998

1 2 3 4 5 6 7 8 9 / 06 05 04 03 02 01 00 99 98

contents

introduction

❖

Peace and tranquillity—that's what most of us want at home. We yearn for a space of our own that is not only pleasing but also signifies who we are, what we like, and even the values we hold. Perhaps we're a little tired of the "stage-set" approach to decorating, which dictates rigid guidelines for specific styles, such as Victorian, Shaker, or even Minimalism. Unlike an article of clothing, which can be worn for a season, then relegated to the back of the closet, our home style surrounds us all of the time. Perhaps we want a look of our own that makes room for the old family hand-me-downs, castoffs, and junkshop finds that most of us start off with, as well as a few new pieces, so that our style is built up, layer upon layer, over the years. And, if we're honest, that's how we want it. But while an unstructured style encourages self-expression, it can also be daunting. Furnishings and decorative objects are far too expensive to scrap and replace if we make mistakes. The key to simple style is to take everything back to basics. This approach aims to make the most of the space and architectural elements of a room, to create environments of quiet, simple elegance, and, by using some easy crafting techniques, to adapt the details of home decor to devise a distinctive look.

The goals of *Simple Home Style* are to help you surmount the hurdle of the "blank canvas," to develop a unique home decor that is flexible enough to accommodate new trends, and to avoid distracting embellishment and clutter. This book presents ideas and instructions for making window treatments and adapting furniture and accessories that suit a simple approach to style. But before beginning a project, the framework of a simple-style room should be considered, in order to explain the thinking behind the look.

CREATING THE CANVAS: WALLS, WINDOWS, FLOORS

Just as with any decorative style, architecture is the starting point for simple home style. However, unlike more proscribed styles, simple style can be adapted to complement the basic design of any structure, whether old or new, rather than obscuring it in distracting colors or patterns. The framework of the room—walls, windows, floors, and ceiling—should provide a "canvas" for the furnishings and accessories. The less complicated the

overall look of this framework, the more tranquil the room will appear, and the best way to achieve simplicity is to assess all of the elements simultaneously. Don't fall victim to distracting design clichés, such as emphasizing certain architectural details with a contrasting color. Either paint all of the surfaces in a single color, or use a color similar to that used for the walls for the baseboards, wainscoting, and picture or crown moldings. In addition, use blinds or basic curtains that leave window frames exposed. The floor is the final piece of the room's "puzzle," though it's not always appropriate to make color the priority in this case, since its practical aspect is the most important. Natural-finish oak or pine floorboards and stone floors are not only durable but have good looks, and can be embellished with kilims and other classic area rugs that are soft underfoot. Floor coverings made of natural materials such as undyed seagrass, sisal, coir, and jute look attractive in high-traffic areas such as hallways, landings, and stairs. If you love the look and comfort of wall-to-wall carpeting, choose a color that suits all the rooms in the house, to provide continuity throughout.

COLOR

Color is critical because it makes the single greatest impact on a room. Lessen the anxiety of making a choice by giving yourself plenty of time. Paint large color swatches on pieces of illustration board and hang them in different parts of the room. Live with the swatches for several days, or even months, until you feel sure that a particular color is right. Our perception of color is greatly affected by the quality of light, which is why it's necessary to examine swatches in several areas of a room, as well as at different times of the day and perhaps through more than one season.

▶ 7

Make sure that colors in adjacent spaces complement each other. Colors of furniture and accessories that you craft or customize will also affect the final outcome. One of the joys of crafting your own decorative items is that your choice of color schemes is far more extensive than if you buy something ready-made. If you're painting, the choices can run into thousands. And even if you're using a fabric that's made in a limited number of colorways, it can be mixed and matched with others in an infinite number of combinations.

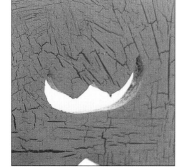

Use color to link dissimilar items visually. Four old kitchen chairs can be made into a set when painted in the same or complementary colors. Another way to use color effectively is to refresh a pretty piece of furniture with a decorative effect such as découpage.

FABRICS AND MATERIALS

Choose natural-fiber fabrics for timeless appeal. Think of crisp cotton, weighty linen, soft wool, shimmering silk. Not only do they all have body, which makes them hang well, but they age beautifully. Plain, functional fabrics such as cotton duck, denim, and old linen sheeting can look wonderful hung at a window with simple tabs, shackles, or ties, without complicated gathers. While bold and busy designs can be distracting in an otherwise simple-style room, there is a place for pattern. Traditional woven checks and stripes work best because they have universal appeal and can be mixed and matched easily and with great success.

Materials for furniture and accessories can be obtained from both conventional and unusual sources. Check out building supply stores for roofing studs and flashing, both of which can be used to finish as well as create pieces, and architectural salvage yards for beautifully aged reclaimed wood.

FURNITURE AND STORAGE

Once the canvas of walls and floor has been prepared, you are ready to choose furniture. Proportion is the most important consideration. Large pieces, for example, can overwhelm a small room, while diminutive ones may look out of place in a large space. If you start by buying items that are in proportion with the dimensions of your rooms, you will find that they naturally go together.

Finding your own style is a matter of taking your time to consider each piece carefully. Does it have pleasing proportions? Does it look balanced? If it's a table or a chair, are its legs long, short, slender, or study enough for the top or seat they support? Will it perform its intended function? Do its decorative details work with the room's existing features? Do you like its color? If you don't, can you change it? Only when all of these questions have been answered to your satisfaction does a piece deserve a place in your home. In general, look for clean, uncluttered lines. An unattractive finish can usually be changed, but there is very little you can do to correct an unattractive shape. Try out as many different kinds and styles of furniture as you can. Choose only comfortable seating: sofas that invite you to sink back; dining room chairs that promise relaxing support for at least the length of a dinner party. Again, it's better to buy old and well-designed pieces that can be reupholstered or slipcovered than to be seduced by a trendy color on a clumsy shape. Simple style means design that is practical as well as good looking. If you have small children, don't let it stop you from buying a cream-colored sofa if you want one, but choose one with removable, machine-washable slipcovers. Regardless of your family's circumstances, simple style also means organizing to keep surfaces and spaces clutter-free, which saves time in the long run. Make room for plenty of storage, and put everything it its place. If you prefer, conceal storage containers such as boxes and baskets inside cabinets and drawers. This strategy will immediately increase storage capacity while sorting things by type or use. Put up plenty of hooks for coats, baskets, and bags. That way, the chore of tidying up (and then finding things) becomes much easier.

ACCESSORIES

Simple-style accessories are usually functional rather than purely ornamental, which can clutter a room and require time-consuming dusting. They also need to relate to the proportions of the furniture and the space, so choose generously sized lamps and vases for large-scale rooms, delicate ones for smaller spaces.

Good design is good design, regardless of a piece's age and style. Many of us are naturally drawn to old favorites, such as traditional blue-and-white dish towels or plain white china, simply because they feature serviceable designs with a pleasing balance that have stood the test of time. Items designed with functional efficiency in mind typically have a beauty that runs deeper than simple good looks. If they are easy to use and perform well, they have an intrinsic balance that attracts the eye. Purchase china and glassware that feel comfortable in your hands; lighting that gives real service; napkins that are generous enough to cover the largest lap; cushions that provide support; and curtains that keep out drafts as well as look good. In short, a happy home is one in which everything functions efficiently and easily. It is also rewarding to design and craft your own furnishings and accessories, or to customize them to suit your taste. This gives you ultimate control over the look of a room.

The combination of balanced proportions, uncomplicated styling, and lack of clutter all add up to home as a tranquil haven. *Simple Home Style* offers inspiration for making soft furnishings and accessories for your home. The projects can be made following the instructions provided, or used as a stimulus to create original designs. True to the concept of simple style, all of the projects in this book are easy to make, so that none is beyond the reach of anyone who has a nodding acquaintance with a sewing machine or a hammer and saw. Most of the designs were influenced by the materials from which they are made.

Nothing is expensive or flamboyant. None of the projects is difficult to make. Yet all retain an elegance that is essentially simple style.

window treatments

▶ 11

C omplement, rather than swamp, windows with fabric. Simple style curtains are part blind, part drape, using a single width of fabric, with just a little extra for movement that can be drawn across the window in the traditional way. Dispensing with elaborate gathering and pinching, simple style curtain headings are tied, looped, hooked, or shackled to poles.

Wherever possible, work with the architecture of the windows. If the curtains can be contained within the window frame, so much the better, as that leaves the features of its casing or trim visible. If the windows are not recessed the poles should reach beyond the frame so that it can be seen when single-width curtains are drawn back during the day.

Using just a single width of fabric makes simple style inexpensive, that lends the look its elegance and the fabric. For main curtains or blinds, Test the weight in your hands them, choose a lighter or darker not only lends a professional look

Natural fabrics handle well and When purchasing fabrics, look beyond

rather than the traditional double and and it is this minimalist treatment shifts the emphasis to the design of use a heavy fabric that will fall well. when buying. If you decide to line value in a linen/cotton blend. This but makes the curtains reversible. will always give the best results. home furnishing departments and

consider fabrics that are not traditionally associated with curtainmaking. Denim, artists' cotton duck or

canvas, old sheets, old tablecloths with fine drawn threadwork at the hems, roller towels or blue-and-white dish towels, and Indian bedspreads are just some of the fabrics that can be transformed into fabulous curtains.

If you like pattern, weaves such as stripes, checks, and Ikats look best with simple style. For details, use different headings, discreet or contrasting topstitching, buttons, studs, and eyelets.

WINDOW TREATMENTS

unstructured
blind

What can be more beautiful than old linen?

Thick and heavy, years of laundering give it a quality that just doesn't exist in new linen. It needs little fuss, as it looks its best when allowed to fall naturally. This wonderful bedroom window treatment is simply made from an old French linen sheet, which has been adapted for this purpose with just two box pleats at the top to fit the width of the window. It is drawn up by three cords threaded through rows of rings at the back, which let the linen fall into its own natural voluptuous folds. The hem of the sheet is turned under and held in position by the first row of rings so the exquisite monogram can be seen whether the blind is up or down.

A large, densely embroidered monogram provides a focus for this unstructured blind.

shackled
heading

Sleek, smart, and vaguely nautical, here is an imaginative window treatment that is elegant in its simplicity. The full-length curtains, made from heavy woven cotton, have been lined edge-to-edge with a plain linen/cotton blend for a smart tailored look.

The curtains have been cut several inches wider than the window to give them just a little movement. They are hung on a sleek polished steel curtain pole with French yachting shackles fed through an eyelet heading.

The top fabric and lining were made the same size for an elegant reversible look.

Look for yachting shackles with smooth elegant lines to create an attractive heading.

glorious
organza

Floaty and feminine, organza has firm body, so it hangs beautifully without relying on gathers. Hang a plain white panel at the window to protect your privacy, or experiment with color for a very different look. By hanging a delicate translucent panel, you can be brave with color, as light can pour through, keeping the tones subtle. Here, two harmonious shades of gold and orange pure silk organza have been stitched together in panels for an elegant ribbon effect. The lightweight organza is offset with robust machine fell seams and double topstitching. The curtain is finished with exquisite shell buttons that fasten the tabs at the front of the curtain.

Shell buttons complement both shades of fabric.

simple
headings

Free from flounce and frill, simple curtain headings can also be the most elegant. Tabs are among the most successful and easy to make, while ties provide a more casual appearance. They require two to three times as much fabric as tabs, but offer far more design possibilities. Make ties slim and self-lined or broaden them into generous contrast-lined "bows," like those shown opposite, for a more decorative treatment.

Fixing eyelets to the top of curtains offers a number of unusual and innovative hanging possibilities. In addition to using shackles (see page 19), you can use butchers' hooks to link curtain to pole. Yacht wire and rope can be threaded through the eyelets and fastened appropriately. For curtains that don't need to be drawn, such as sheers, hook them straight onto a line of cuphooks fixed into the window frame, or simply fasten curtain clips to the top of the curtain. You can also apply this idea to blinds by adding a row of eyelets to the hem. Just hook the bottom of the blind onto the cuphooks to let light into the room.

d e n i m
c u r t a i n

Denim is a fabric with enduring appeal. Associated with a casual robustness, it is a material that many fashion designers are now using in their sportswear lines. Put denim at your window, and immediately the room has a relaxed appearance. Denim can be mixed and matched with most traditional household linens, and, like jeans, can be dressed up or down. Choose a pale blue denim and wash it before making it into curtains—this will preshrink and soften it. Faithful to conventional jeans detailing, this curtain features double-line topstitching and metal rivet buttons. This no-fuss fabric demands a no-fuss fixture—any wooden pole will suffice.

Using jeans rivets and the combination of double and single topstitching echoes the design of traditional jeans.

▶ 29

A cushion's *raison d'etre* is to invite you to sit down, relax, and generally make yourself at home. Although cushions seem to play a bit part in the general scheme of a room, they can influence its appearance. Just by changing the cushions, you can quickly transform the mood of an interior. When generously sized and lavishly scattered, cushions convey a relaxed mood, while smaller and more tailored designs offer a more businesslike look. Cushions can also have an impact on the color of a room, by providing accents of color that can successfully integrate its various elements.

The design of a cushion can also contribute to the overall interior style. For a simple look, the emphasis shifts from tassels and fancy trimmings to a clever use of fabrics and discreet detailing. Covers may be buttoned or tied, incorporate subtle color, or make use of topstitching. A simple, unadorned cushion cover takes on a more tailored appearance when two lines of topstitching are sewn around its edge. Sew the same two rows of topstitching further in and you have yet another look.

One of the great advantages of making your own cushions, rather than buying them ready-made, is the variety of fabrics, colors, and trimmings available, offering unlimited possibilities for design. Colors can be teamed with any number of different trimmings or stitching treatments. Choose two or three coordinating fabrics with similar characteristics for a sophisticated color scheme. Natural fabrics such as crisp linen, pure cotton, and even fine wool always produce a classic look. And you don't have to restrict yourself to furnishing fabrics. The cushions in this chapter, for instance, are made from dressweight linen, which offers an irresistibly subtle choice of colors.

CUSHIONS

buttoned-up cushion

Elegantly tailored in the softest blue linen and trimmed with four generous mother-of-pearl buttons, the appeal of this cushion cover design lies in its simplicity. The buttons are more than just an attractive embellishment—they are working fastenings. The cover has been lined with contrasting ecru linen to give it the sophistication of a well-cut suit. Put together like an envelope-style pillowcase, this cover is easy to remove for cleaning. For a different, yet equally beautiful look, choose a coarser-weave linen teamed with bone or wooden buttons.

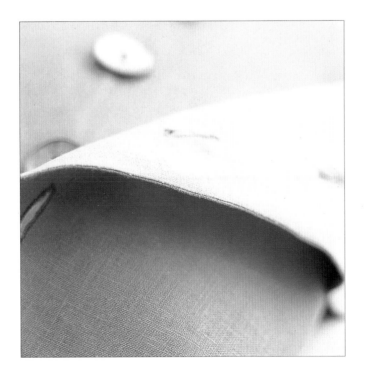

Working buttons offer a practical solution for laundering while providing an elegant trim.

tied
cushion

Here is another cushion for which the fastening has become the focal point of the design. Ties can be made large and bold like this, or slim and discreet, mimicking a traditional continental pillowcase. The cushion cover is made with a contrasting facing that heightens visual interest.

The choice of fabrics has a strong influence on the style—had it been lined with a floral print, it would have taken on a country look, while a bright color would have lent modern tones. The neutral lining shown here gives the cushion a classic elegance.

Ties offer a relaxed mode of fastening that can also become a focal point of the design.

CUSHIONS

cushion trims

Trims and details give cushions their personality. Make them fun and flirty with a row of coquettish lime bobbles like this, or opt for restrained elegance with simple piping. Keep in mind that the choice of trim color can have a huge influence on the finished effect. The same bobble trim in powder blue on this blue cushion, for example, would have lent an altogether more subtle look. Even classic piping can be used to make a design statement, depending on the choice of color. By choosing piping in the same or a similar color, cushions influence the design of the room simply by their color and size. Pipe them in a contrasting color, and cushions become more sophisticated, bringing a more geometric and city-feel to the overall look of the interior. Trim doesn't necessarily have to be purchased. You can make your own, by cutting a scalloped or zigzag border in the same fabric, for example, and sewing it into the cushion seam, for a pretty yet elegant look.

secret
color

Subtle yet smart, the trim on this cushion is an integral part of the design. Ostensibly a simple ecru-colored cushion, it has double topstitched flanges that conceal a blue lining. Plumped up on a sofa, it offers subtle flashes of blue. Adapt this idea to any color scheme and make cushions with as many shades as you like, chosen from the accent colors of the room. With such understated elegance, each one can be given a different shade, lending accent without becoming busy.

CUSHIONS

N ot many of us start with a clean slate—we're usually pretty grateful for a few hand-me-down pieces of furniture when we set up our first home. But by choosing simple style, furniture of all kinds and ages can be mixed and matched. The trick is to retain a sense of proportion. Buy pieces that suit the scale of your home, and you'll find they all have a sense of belonging when they're put together. Another tip is to believe in your own sense of style. Ask yourself if you really like a piece of furniture before you buy it. Reject any piece that isn't quite right, even in the smallest detail. A good guideline is to look for simplicity—strong, simple lines are always elegant and won't detract from the basic proportions and design in the same way that elaborate ornamentation can. Classic designs do not go out of fashion and can look good in virtually any decor. It is easy to become sidetracked by fancy details in a store, only to find when you bring the piece home, its proportions are wrong and there is little you can do to improve it. But if you buy a piece with pleasing proportions, you can always add a touch of paint or some other finish to bring it in keeping with

the rest of the furniture in the house. A disparate collection of old kitchen chairs can work well when they share a common color (or even a series of complementary colors). An attractively shaped but battered old table can be given a new lease on life when the legs are given a touch of paint or colored wax and the top is "pickled" with a coat of

zinc white paint. And it may be a cliché, but it is still better to buy a comfy old sofa that has attractive lines and is well made, even if the covers are worn out, than to compromise on a new one with inferior proportions that will never live up to the job of providing comfort at the end of a long day. An attractive throw on an old sofa can always do the interim job of marrying looks with comfort until you can have it recovered.

FURNITURE

crackle-glazed chairs

With their pretty, classic French shape, these rush-seated chairs were a great bargain-find at about the cost of a pizza each. Their high-gloss cream finish didn't do them justice, but renovating them with a soft Scandinavian blue paint-effect gave them fresh appeal. To add interest, the legs and cross struts were crackle-glazed in slightly different shades from the rest of the chair. This technique looks good on many types of furniture—chests, tables, china closets, and even with the same shade of paint for the top coat. Alternative effects can be achieved by using different undercoats. The simplest option is to use a dark undercoat with a top coat in a lighter value of the same color.

mosaic
cabinet

This delightful simple-style turtle mosaic brings charm and interest to an unassuming bathroom cabinet. The unusual combination of brick red, sage green, and blue matte-finish tiles are set off by the iridescent glass tiles of the turtle's shell. Mosaic is not difficult to do, and the permanence of this craft lends a quality that seems to make even the least significant pieces of furniture become part of the architecture. Here, the choice of an aquatic creature, the amphibious turtle set within a classic keyline border, brings wit to the most watery room in the house.

The green iridescent tiles of the turtle's shell, introduced as a contrast to the mainly matte finish, lend extra dimension to the whole piece.

FURNITURE

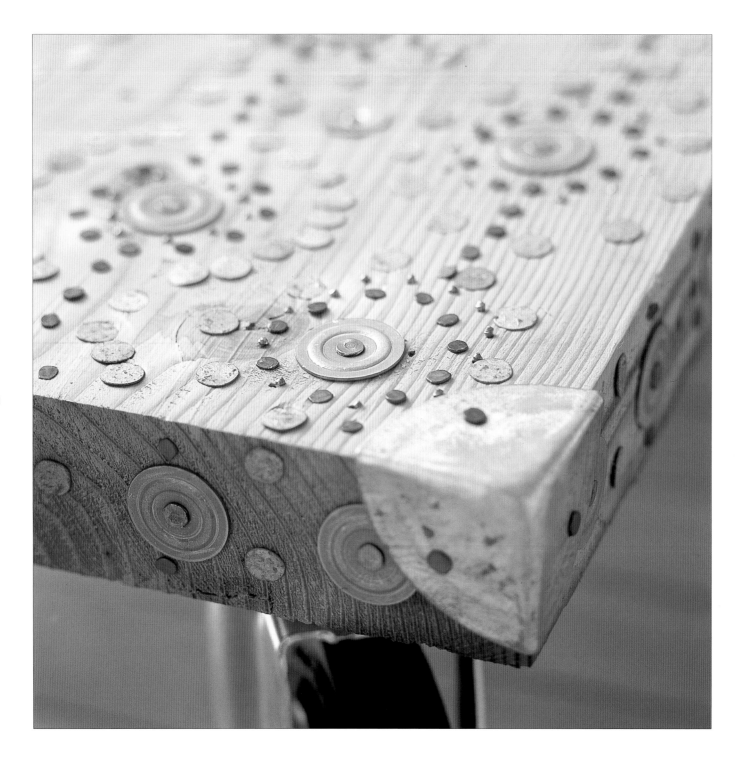

studded coffee table

Roofing studs, nails, and tacks are unlikely decorative materials, but the combination of copper, steel, and galvanized metal gives this coffee table a wonderfully contemporary appearance. The nail heads come in a wide variety of sizes, offering plenty of design options. This glorious wavy pattern against the grainy wood surface, finished off by metal corners and easy-to-fit wheels that double as legs, turns a couple of unassuming joists into a dramatically simple coffee table. For a more restrained pattern, the studs and nails could have been positioned in rows or squares. The same idea can be adapted to update uninspired cabinets, tables, and storage units.

▶ 49

A combination of zinc and copper stud and nail heads make for an attractive color scheme.

metallic-effect cabinet

Stripes and checks in shades of bronze, brass, and copper bring a simple cabinet to life in an original way. By using vertical stripes in a range of widths rather than following the lines of its elements exactly, the cabinet takes on more elegant proportions. You don't need the skill of an artist to master this decorative technique, just the ability to mix metallic powdered pigments with paint for a delightful sheen and the judicious placement of masking tape to make straight stripes. Echoing simple-style fabric patterns, stripes, lines, and checks can be used in any number of combinations of size, value, or color to complement existing color schemes. Use colors with plenty of contrast for a dramatic effect, or several similar tones for a subtle look.

The checkerboard border around the glass panel is easy to achieve with a stencil.

découpage
chest

Recycled paper and glue is all you need to give an old chest a new look. Tear the paper into squares and strips to create an infinite number of designs. Paste on shapes layer upon layer until you are happy with the overall effect. The joy of this technique is that you can embellish as little or as much as you want, holding up the next motif to try out the look before committing yourself to gluing it in place. And if worse comes to worst and you don't like the results, just continue adding papers. Once you're happy with the design, finish it with a coat of varnish, which will protect the surface as well as bring a wonderful translucency to the whole piece. This découpage design has a sampler feel, but for a simpler style, just repeat the same pattern on all the drawers.

The simple checkerboard top in light-value colors makes an attractive design.

▶ 59

A beautiful lamp, an elegant mirror, a stunning framed piece of art, rugs, mats, bowls, and jugs: these are the things that turn a house into a home. And you can enjoy all of them all the more if you have been selective and there are fewer of them.

Art always lends personality to a room—and is all the more special for being carefully chosen. Don't be urged into buying art simply because a wall needs to be filled. Better to leave the walls bare, waiting for the right piece, or to carefully display just one favorite piece, than to jumble several that are disparate.

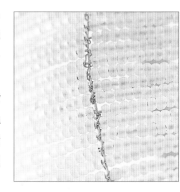

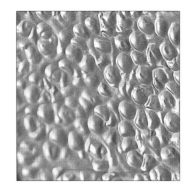

A vase of fresh flowers is always lovely too, linking the interior to the outdoors. Don't try to be elaborate, using wire or foam to support their stems. Just put a generous bunch in a simple vase, and let them fall naturally—they always look more pleasing that way, because it imitates the way they grow.

Display shelves of trinkets and collections that need to be constantly dusted and rearranged require a lot of upkeep, and their small scale can be distracting. If you pare down to functional items, you will automatically clear the decks of clutter.

That is not to say you have to do away with display. If you have casseroles and dishes in wonderful shapes, why not display them on open kitchen shelves? That way, you can enjoy them daily and have them at hand, just where you want them. If they're used regularly they won't collect dust, since you'll be washing them up anyway. If they do, they might as well be put away. Displaying everyday china in a decorative way has a long tradition. That was exactly the function of old cabinets in farmhouse kitchens, which were both functional and brought a homey, decorative feel to the hub of the household.

ACCESSORIES

beaded
lampshade

The translucent texture of frosted beads on wire, wound around and around to make a lampshade, catches the light even when the lamp is off. When it is turned on, it positively sparkles! The slim conical shape on a simple curvy metal lampstand has an elegant '50s look and brings an interesting sculptural element to the room.

The method of threading beads onto wire, then coiling them into a shape, is inspired by traditional African neckwear and can be applied to all manner of accessories, from baskets and bowls to placemats and coasters, using different sizes and colors of beads to create different effects.

▶ 63

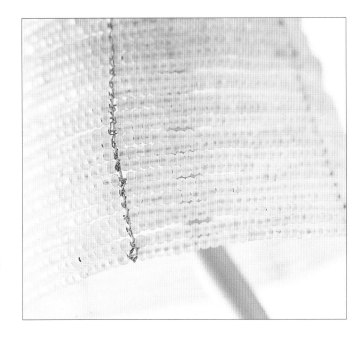

Delicate translucent beads are threaded onto wire, then shaped around a cone in an operation that is not difficult but requires careful manipulation.

hammered
mirror frame

It is often the more prosaic materials around us that prove to be the most interesting when applied in a new way. This striking mirror frame has been covered with humble roofing flashing, then beaten to create a hammered effect. This technique can be used to give a new finish to other items, too, such as cabinet panels or borders. Since flashing comes in strips no more than 6 inches wide, it works best when used on small sections.

The simpler and less embellished any design is, the harder the proportions need to work. Without the disguising effect of decoration, any incongruous dimensions will be glaringly obvious. Much of the elegance of this mirror lies in its proportions—a perfect square with a generous frame that is almost as wide as its center panel.

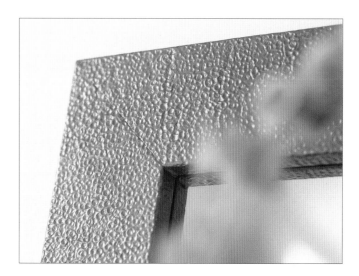

Hammered roofing flashing provides a handsome finish for a mirror frame.

ACCESSORIES

painted
floorcloth

❖

An easy—and inexpensive—way to find a floor covering in exactly the colors you want is to paint one yourself. Painted on artists' cotton duck canvas, floorcloths look wonderful on bare floorboards, and simple geometric designs bring them right up to date. Quite apart from their pleasing looks, geometrics are a wise choice because you don't need to be an artist to achieve great results. Featuring two values of the same color in a classic checkerboard design, this floorcloth will have lasting appeal. Paint it in your favorite shades; when you're ready for a change, just sand it down, apply an undercoat, then paint it in a new set of colors.

d r i f t w o o d
b a t h m a t

The wonderful, weathered gray tones of driftwood are often difficult to resist...and small pieces like these are easy to find on riverbanks as well as on the beach. So here is a bathmat that is free, except for the cost of leather thong to string the driftwood pieces together. More comfortable to stand on than it may at first appear, a lifetime by the sea makes the driftwood more than able to cope with a few splashes of bath water. And when you've finished your bath or shower, it can be hung up to drain.

Driftwood and natural leather thong make a delightful combination of textures.

A row of toggles at each end provide charming detail.

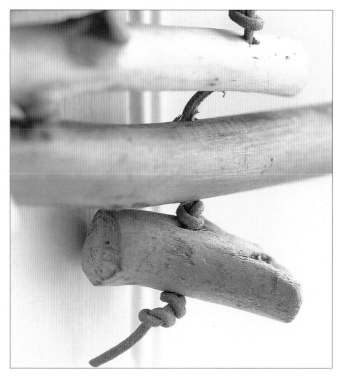

linens

▶ 71

D ining areas are often naturally simple, with the focus on the table and chairs in the middle of the room. What great opportunity linens offer! Change the linens, and you can change the whole personality of the room. There's little that can beat a white damask tablecloth for a formal dinner; exchange it for a cool modern geometric for lunch, or bright placemats for a family snack. Table linens need not be expensive—even two humble blue-and-white dish towels sewn together can look fabulous, fresh, and inviting. If you want to entertain large numbers and plan to push two tables together to make one that is far too large for any of your cloths, look in the linen closet for sheets with drawn threadwork hems, bedspreads, or throws.

Making your own table linens is neither difficult, nor necessarily expensive, especially if you choose inexpensive fabrics, such as heavy Indian cotton, cotton duck, light-weight canvas, denim, and muslin. Even if you don't consider yourself a whiz on the sewing machine, you should be able to manage since table linen at its most basic requires only a hem around the edge of the fabric.

If you have a fine wooden table, you may prefer to do without a tablecloth, though you're likely to need napkins and placemats. For simple style, either will do. For placemats, choose fabrics in solid colors or with interesting weaves that can be finished with a contrasting fabric trim. Fringes and tassels are likely to be distracting, so embellish

instead with neat mitered edges, blocks of color or simple appliqué. Blanket stitch is an effective edging for brightly colored mats, especially if they're made of a thicker fabric such as felt or polar fleece. Topstitching is a very useful finish for finer linens. One row of stitches is neat and understated; two or three give a defined edge, lending a sophisticated elegance.

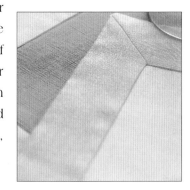

LINENS

o r g a n d y
t a b l e c l o t h

❖

The breathtaking charm of this delightful organdy tablecloth lies in its simplicity. Light and sheer, it veils the table, lending it a "dressed" look and sense of importance without concealing its pretty shape. Glass beads sewn around the hem at wide intervals add weight to the fabric. The organdy and glass beads work well together because they are so similar in translucency and color, so neither overshadows the other. Had the beads been more colorful, they could have been distracting. The finished cloth offers the perfect decorative detail for a summer dessert table or a christening tea. This idea could also be adapted for a table runner, where the longer droplets could be sewn along the short ends.

▶ 75

Droplets of six beads trim the corners, while groups of threes finish off the sides.

stunningly simple
placemats

An elegant mitered border is all you need to design an infinite number of placemat variations, providing color schemes for every occasion. These placemats are made from an inexpensive heavy Indian cotton that comes in a rainbow of colors. Make up matching mats or choose two or three colors that work well and mix the combinations to create a coordinated though not uniform look. Colors can vary widely in appearance, depending on the colors they are used with and the proportions in which they are used. The yellow in both these mats is the same fabric, though it looks more lemony next to the lime and more banana-toned with the tangerine. The unfussy design would complement any simple style. Choose these muted citrus shades for a fresh modern approach, elegant neutrals for a classic look, and pale muted gray-blues and gray-greens for a peaceful Scandinavian feel.

fishy appliqué
tablecloth

Clean, uncluttered appliqué shapes, such as these
fish and reeds, bring a fresh new look to traditional
appliqué. The juxtaposition of aqua with bright yellow
offers a light, bright, modern feel, and the two-color
design provides a useful way to incorporate the joining of fabric widths to make up whatever size tablecloth you need. Appliqué can be used in many forms
for table linen. An appliqué zigzag or scalloped border
in a contrasting color can look very stylish, as can
applying a single motif, such as a leaf or a triangle, to
the corner of a napkin that coordinates with a similar
but larger motif on the tablecloth. When unusual colors
like these are used, the tablecloth makes a strong
design statement in itself, so take care when choosing
the colors for your napkins.

The fish are made up in two
parts—a body and a tail—and
small scraps of fabric are used to
decorate them.

felt
placemats

Thick fabrics such as felt provide excellent protection for table surfaces against hot plates. Simply blanket-stitch the edges in a contrasting thread for fun yet stylish mats. If desired, add some lively primitive-style motifs such as a simple bird silhouette. By choosing three coordinating colors, each mat and bird can be different and each member of the family can have his or her own. A more contemporary warm fabric that can be used for placemats is polar fleece, which is available in a wide variety of colors. Group several colors together and edge them with blanket stitching, or make up two of the brighter colors in a checker-board design for a sophisticated look. Both polar fleece and machine-washable wool are easily laundered, making them practical as well as fun.

Simple felt shapes can be applied using traditional blanket stitch. Use a contrasting color for a stronger visual effect.

putting it together

T here's something immensely satisfying about making your own furnishings and accessories for the home. It has to do with the flexibility of choice. In home decorating and furniture stores, every

item comes in a limited range of colors; when you make something yourself, you have an endless variety of fabrics and colors to choose from. With so much choice, you can put together exactly what you want; add detail where you want it, leave it out if you prefer. It is all part of the design process, and by making something yourself, you're taking greater control, adjusting and adapting to suit your needs.

There's a thrill in having an idea, of finding and buying the materials; and the excitement of anticipation about how it will turn out.

None of the items in this book is difficult to make. They are all designed to be easy; most are quick, but there are one or two that require a little more tinkering, such as the beaded lampshade and the mosaic cabinet. None should be too taxing for anyone who enjoys crafting. The projects are also chosen to inspire; to perhaps stimulate a variation on the theme that would perhaps suit your home or style even better.

The key to whatever you make is in the choice of materials, the combi-

nation of colors and textures. Try always to use natural materials, which will stand the test of time and handle better. Pared down simple style does not rely on expensive trimmings and embellishments or even large quantities of fabric, so you can afford to purchase good-quality materials. If you research sources imaginatively, they don't need to be costly. Look in unexpected places, such as antique stores and flea markets, the fabric sections of department stores, art supply stores, and fabric retailers. You may even find materials in hardware and home improvement stores, lumberyards, ship chandlers, and stores that sell furniture and accessories.

PUTTING IT TOGETHER

unstructured blind

❖

The success of this glorious window treatment is the weight of the linen sheet from which it is made. If you can't find a suitable sheet, good-quality linen bought off the roll is a good substitute.

MEASURING UP

This treatment is designed to hang inside the window frame. To determine fabric quantities, measure the width and length of the window. Add an extra 6in/15cm to the length and 2in/5cm to the width for seams. This is the absolute minimum requirement for the fabric. If you have a piece that is larger, so much the better. The maximum length you need is about one and a half times the length of the window.

The blind is gathered up by cords that are threaded through brass rings at the back. Since each blind needs to be made to measure, you may like to try out the positions with safety pins to make sure you're happy with the finished look before you start sewing on the rings.

MATERIALS

◆ *Fabric to the required measurements*
◆ *A 2 x 1in/5 x 2.5cm piece of wood cut to fit within the window frame*
◆ *Muslin to cover the wood*
◆ *Staple gun or upholstery tacks*
◆ *Measuring tape*
◆ *Small brass rings to make three vertical rows about 10in/25cm apart*
◆ *As many safety pins as rings*
◆ *Four large screw eyes*
◆ *Sewing thread*
◆ *Non-stretch cord that is three times the sum of the length plus the width of the blind*
◆ *Blind pull*
◆ *Angle irons*
◆ *One cleat*

1 Cut a piece of muslin to cover the wood support, allowing sufficient fabric for turnings. Turn in the raw edges and staple into position on one narrow edge.

2 Cut the blind fabric to the size of your measurements. Turn in and sew any raw edges.

3 Ensure that any features, such as a monogram, are centered close to the bottom edge where they will be seen.

4 Place the blind right side down on a flat surface.

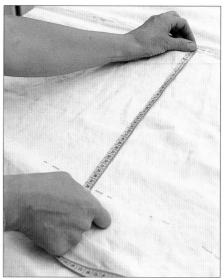

5 Down the length of fabric, measure and mark the center line using pins. Measure and mark the halfway point between the center and left-hand edge. Repeat for the right-hand edge.

6 Sew a brass ring close to the bottom edge of the fabric, at each of the three marked points.
(See picture next column)

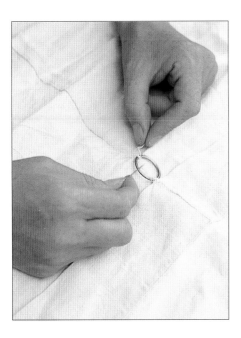

8 Staple the top edge of the blind to a 1in/2.5cm edge of the wood support. If the fabric is too wide, make box pleats to fit at intervals.

11 Cut the cord into three equal lengths. Tie one end to each of the bottom three rings. Thread the cord up through the rings, along the support through the screw eyes to the screw eye at the end of the blind. Gather the lengths together, thread them through the blind pull. Trim the cords to equal lengths and make a knot at the bottom. Fix the support to the wall using the angle irons. Screw the cleat to the window frame on the same side as the extra screw eye. Pull up the blind and secure the cords in the cleat.

7 On each marked line, measure 10in/25cm from the first ring and stitch on another. Repeat up the length. Leave a 16in/40cm gap between the last two.

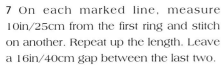

9 Fix three screw eyes to the 2in/5cm wide underside of the wood support in line with the position of each of the three rows of rings.

10 Fix another screw eye at one end of the support through which all the cords will be threaded.

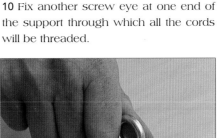

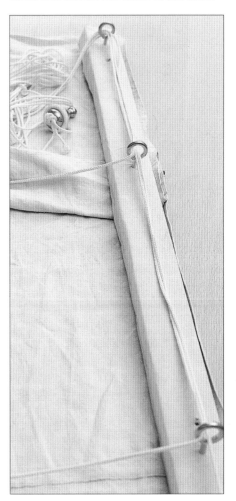

shackled heading

❖

The eyelets are carefully placed so that they always fall on a cream stripe, giving the curtains a smart tailored look and emphasizing the unusual heading. Eyelets are easy to find in fabric and notions stores and are usually sold in packs complete with their own assembly tool.

MEASURING UP

These curtains are fitted to the outside of the window frame. For a pair of curtains, measure the full width of the frame and add 8in/20cm to allow for two finials plus 4in/10cm for seam allowances. Halve this final figure to determine the width you need to cut for each curtain. The length is from the curtain rail to the floor or the windowsill as preferred, plus 4in/10cm for hems.

MATERIALS

◆ *Heavy curtain fabric to the length calculated*
◆ *Linen/cotton blend fabric for lining to the length calculated*
◆ *Tape measure*
◆ *Pins*
◆ *Four curtain weights*

◆ *Lightweight fabric scraps*
◆ *Dressmaking scissors*
◆ *Sewing thread*
◆ *Eyelets (internal diameter ½in/1cm)— allow at least one per every 8in/20cm*
◆ *Hammer*
◆ *One yachting shackle for each eyelet*

1 Measure the fabric. Cut two curtains in the main fabric and two linings.

2 From scraps cut squares large enough to make four pockets for the weights.

3 To make the pockets, place two squares right sides together. Stitch three sides, turn right side out, place the weight in, and slipstitch to close. Make four.

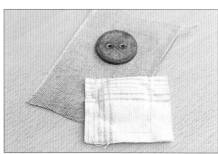

4 Place one curtain on a flat surface, right side up. Place a lining right side down on top. Pin together. Start at the top of one long edge and stitch down the length, across the width at the bottom and up the second length.

5 Trim the seams and press open. Snip off the corners. Stitch one weight to the lining at each bottom corner.

6 Turn the curtain right side out. Turn in the top raw edges and slipstitch to close. Press.

7 Mark the positions for the eyelets and fix them in place using the assembling tool and a hammer. Place a shackle through each eyelet. Repeat for the second curtain.

glorious organza

❖

This delightful sheer curtain has been made in five alternating bands of two contrasting colors. You can adapt the number of bands and the width of each to suit the size of your window.

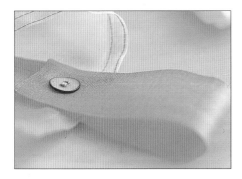

MEASURING UP

This single curtain is fitted to the outside of the window frame. Measure the full width of the frame and add 8in/20cm to allow for two finials and another 12in/30cm for seams. Decide how many panels you want and divide the width of the curtain by the number of panels to determine how wide each panel will be. The length is from the curtain rail to the floor or windowsill as preferred, plus 4in/20cm for hems. Allow an extra 4in/10cm for tabs.

MATERIALS

◆ *Correct length of two colors of silk organza*
◆ *Scissors*
◆ *Measuring tape*
◆ *Pins*
◆ *Sewing thread in the main color*
◆ *One shell button for each tab*

1 Divide the width of the curtain measurement evenly to determine the width of the panels. An odd number of panels will look better and you can have the main color on both outside edges. If the figure does not divide neatly, make the curtain slightly wider.

2 For each panel, allow 1in/2.5cm on each side for seams. Cut out the panels.

3 Cut one tab for each panel plus one extra, measuring 2 x 6in/5 x 15cm. Fold the tabs in half lengthways, right sides together. Stitch across one short edge and along the long raw edge. Trim the seams and turn right side out. Position the seam at one side. Press.

4 Arrange the panels on a flat surface in alternating colors. Pin, then stitch together using fell seams.

5 Turn in the raw edge of each tab. Pin this end to each side of the curtain top and one to the top of each seam joining the panels. Baste. Taking in the tabs as you go, machine a double hem all around the curtain, making a double line of topstitching.

6 Bring the loose end of the tab to the front. Center a button on the tab and sew it on through all thicknesses.

denim curtain

❖

Denim is a tight-woven fabric that does not need to be lined. Unless your window is very wide, it looks good as a single curtain that can simply be drawn to one side.

MEASURING UP

This treatment hangs inside the window reveal if there is one, so measure the width and length of the window. Add an extra 6in/15cm to the length and 3in/7.5cm to the width for hems and seams. You will also need an extra ½yd/0.5m for the tab tops. Wash the denim before you begin to pre-shrink it and to soften the fabric. Jeans' rivets are easy to find in fabric and notions stores and often are available as kits with their own assembling tools.

MATERIALS
◆ *Denim to measurements required*
◆ *Measuring tape*
◆ *Scissors*
◆ *Pins*
◆ *Yellow thread*
◆ *Jeans' rivets*
◆ *Hammer*

1 Cut the curtain to the size of your measurements.

2 Allow one tab for every 12in/30cm of the width. To make each tab cut one piece 13 x 4in/33 x 10cm. Fold in half lengthways, right sides together. Stitch the long sides and one short side. Press the seams open. Trim the seams and corners. Turn right side out. Turn in the raw edges and slipstitch to close. Press. Topstitch all around each tab.

3 Turn in the seams around the raw edges of the curtain. Press. Pin the tabs at equal intervals to the wrong side of the top of the curtain. Baste.

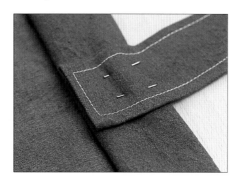

4 Double topstitch all around the curtain, taking in the tabs.

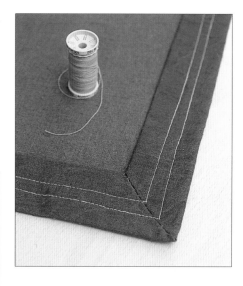

5 Turn the free ends of the tabs to the curtain front and attach the rivets using the assembly tool and hammer.

buttoned-up cushion

❖

Mother-of-pearl buttons add texture and visual interest to this easy-to-make cushion. Designed like an envelope-style pillowcase, the facings are in contrasting ecru linen, giving it a well-finished, tailored look.

MATERIALS

- *Cushion pad 12in/30cm square*
- *¹/₂yd/50cm blue linen*
- *¹/₂yd/50cm ecru linen*
- *Four mother-of-pearl buttons 1in/2.5cm diameter*
- *Blue thread*

1 From blue, for the cushion front cut one 15in/38cm square. Cut one cushion back 22 x 15in/56 x 38cm.

2 From ecru, cut one lining 15in/38cm square. Cut one lining 15 x 7in/38 x 18cm.

3 Turn in a double hem along one 15in/38cm edge on each ecru piece.

4 Stitch the opposite 15in/38cm raw edge of the smaller ecru lining to the

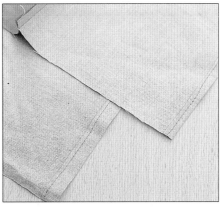

blue square. Press. Fold on the seam line so that wrong sides are together.

5 Place the blue rectangle wrong side down, on a flat surface.

6 On top, at one end, place the blue and ecru panel. Align raw edges. Pin.

7 Place the remaining ecru square right side down on top, aligning raw edges with the other end of the blue rectangle. Pin. There will be four layers of fabric at the center of the rectangle—blue rectangle, blue square, folded-over ecru lining and ecru square.

8 Ensure all raw edges and the two hemmed edges of ecru are aligned. Baste around the raw edges.

9 Stitch around all four sides of the cushion, reinforcing the stitching over the overlap. Trim or overcast the seams. Remove the pins and basting stitches. Snip the corners off within the

seam allowance to reduce bulk. Turn right side out. Press.

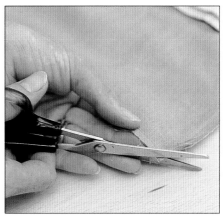

10 Position four buttons at equal intervals across the width of the cushion with their centers 3¹/₂in/9cm from the top edge of the blue square. Stitch each in position.

11 Fold the top flap down. Mark the corresponding position of the buttonholes. Machine stitch buttonholes to finish.

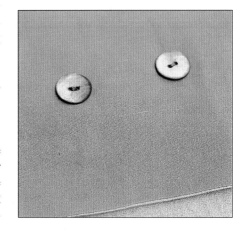

tied cushion

❖

The closures for this cushion cover become a design element when the inside facings and tie backings are stitched in contrasting fabric.

MATERIALS
- ◆ 1/2yd/50cm blue linen
- ◆ 12in/30cm ecru linen
- ◆ Scissors
- ◆ Sewing thread
- ◆ Pins

1 Cut two 15in/38cm squares from blue linen.

2 Cut two 15 x 8in/38cm x 20cm rectangles from ecru linen.

3 Cut four strips of blue and four strips of ecru linen 20 x 3½in/50 x 9cm for the ties.

4 Fold the top left corner of each tie down and trim away. Place one blue and one ecru tie right sides together. Stitch down the long edges and across the diagonal. Trim the seams and turn right sides out. Press. Make four.

5 Turn in and stitch a hem along one long side of each ecru rectangle.

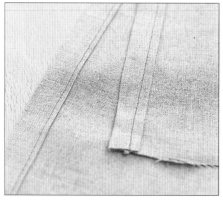

6 With pins, mark into thirds one side of one blue square. Place the marked up blue square right side down on a flat surface.

7 Find the center of the raw edge of two ties and mark with pins. Match the pins with those on the cushion side, and place blue side down. Align raw edges. Place one ecru rectangle on top. Stitch through all layers on this edge.
(*See picture next column*)

8 Press the seam open. Repeat with the other side of the cushion.

9 With right sides together and matching ecru sections, stitch along the cushion side, including the facing, along the short edge and the long edge. Press the seams open. Trim the seams and clip the corners. Turn right side out. Press.

10 Turn the facings in. Place the cushion in the cover, tucking it under one of the ecru facings. Tie to close.

secret color

❖

A simple centered opening on the back means the cover can be removed without putting a strain on the flange trim.

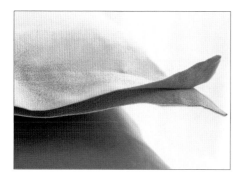

MATERIALS

◆ 1yd/1m ecru linen
◆ ½yd/0.5m blue linen
◆ Ecru thread
◆ Cushion pad 12in/30cm square

1 From ecru, cut one square 19 x 19in/48 x 48cm. Cut two rectangles 12 x 19in/30 x 48cm. Stitch a double hem along one long edge of each rectangle.

2 From blue, cut eight strips 19 x 4in/ 48 x 10cm.

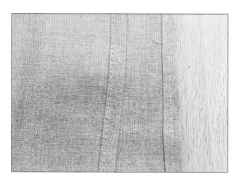

3 Miter each end of each blue strip. Stitch together to make two "frames." Press the seams open. (For directions on making miters see the simple placemats on page 107.)

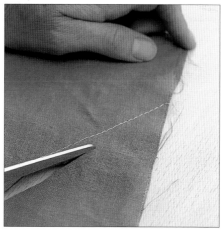

4 To make the cushion back to the correct size, place the ecru square right side down on a flat surface. On top, position the two ecru rectangles right side down and raw edges aligned. Overlap the rectangles at the center. Pin, then baste the overlap.

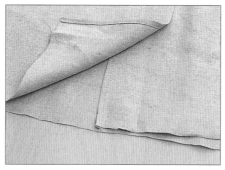

5 Separate the cushion pieces. Place one blue frame and the cushion front right sides together. Stitch around the outer edge. Repeat with the cushion back. Turn right sides out. Press.

6 Place the two sides of the cushion wrong sides together. Topstitch together through all thicknesses 2in/5cm from the edge around all sides. For emphasis, make another line of topstitching ¼in/6cm just outside this.

crackle·glazed chairs

❖

It is not difficult to create a crackle effect using products from a home improvement store. This easy-to-apply technique can be used to decorate and transform all types of wooden furniture with different intensities of "crackle."

MATERIALS
◆ *Wooden chairs*
◆ *Sandpaper—medium and fine grades*
◆ *Masking tape*
◆ *Acrylic primer*
◆ *Selection of small brushes*
◆ *Eggshell-finish latex paints—at least one darker shade for the first coat and a lighter version for the top coat*
◆ *Similar colors in a flat finish but in paler shades*
◆ *Premixed polyester resin filler*
◆ *One paint jar for each color*
◆ *Hair dryer*

1 Prepare the chairs by sanding down the old finish. Remove any loose or flaky paint.

2 Fill any splits or holes. Let dry, then sand down any rough edges.

3 Mask off any areas not intended for painting.

4 Brush on a coat of acrylic primer and let dry.

5 Brush on a coat of the darker shade. Let dry.

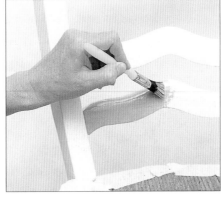

6 Lightly sand the darker coat, then paint over with a lighter shade.

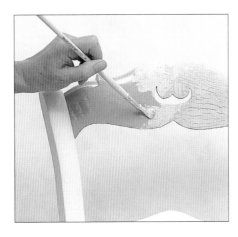

7 As soon as this is applied, quickly combine two parts flat latex with one part polyester resin filler.

8 Brush onto the chair while the lighter coat is still tacky.

9 Apply heat immediately with a hair-dryer and the crackles will appear.

10 Let dry thoroughly. Sand all the surfaces to give a distressed look.

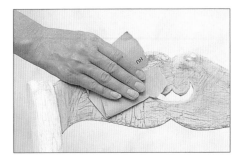

11 Using a different base and top coat, repeat the process on different parts of the chair.

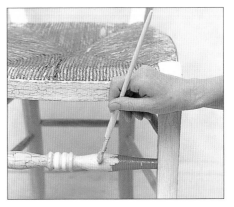

studded coffee table

❖

Nails, studs, and tacks from a hardware store make inexpensive decoration for a simple coffee table. This table is made from recycled floor joists with wheels for legs.

MATERIALS
◆ *Two hardwood floor joists or similar 36in/90cm long*
◆ *150 galvanized metal and/or copper roofing studs*
◆ *650 clout nails*
◆ *500 steel tacks*
◆ *500 copper hardboard pins*
◆ *Hammer*
◆ *Four metal box corners 1 1/2in/38mm*
◆ *Twelve tacks to fix the corners*
◆ *Plywood board 2 1/2 x 8in/6 x 20cm*
◆ *Twelve screws 1 1/2in/38mm*
◆ *Electric drill*
◆ *Four castor wheels 6in/15cm and screws to fix them*

1 To decorate the top surface of the hardwood, hammer in the roofing studs 4in/10cm apart in three rows down the length of each board.
(See next column)

2 Next, hammer in the clout nails, making a circle of about twelve nails around each roofing stud.

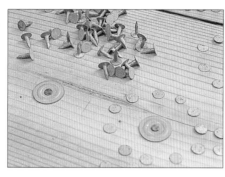

3 Hammer in the steel tacks in a circle inside the clout nails.

4 Finally, hammer in the hardboard pins. Decorate the sides in a similar way.

5 Place the boards right side down, on a protected surface. Center the plywood on top. Make holes for the screws, then screw to secure.

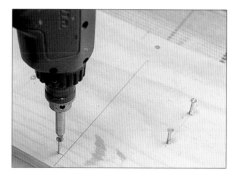

▶ 95

6 Place a wheel at one corner and screw into position. Add the remaining three wheels.

7 Screw the metal corners in place.

mosaic cabinet

❖

Mosaics are not difficult to do. The easiest method is to combine adhesive and grout, for a quick drying formula.

MATERIALS
◆ *Square cabinet 14 x 14in/35 x 35cm*
◆ *Tracing paper*
◆ *Pencil and fine felt-tipped pen*
◆ *Cardboard*
◆ *One 12 x 12in/30 x 30cm sheet of iridescent green glass mosaic tiles*
◆ *One 12 x 12in/30 x 30cm sheet of copper glass mosaic tiles*
◆ *Three 5 x 5in/12 x 12cm sheets of blue matte-finish mosaic tiles*
◆ *Three 5 x 5in/12 x 12cm sheets of terracotta matte-finish mosaic tiles*
◆ *Four 5 x 5in/12 x 12cm sheets of gray-white matte-finish mosaic tiles*
◆ *Spring-loaded tile nippers*
◆ *Tweezers and pliers*
◆ *Mixture of ceramic wall tile adhesive and grout*
◆ *Small round-ended kitchen knife*
◆ *Goggles*
◆ *Sandpaper*
◆ *Palette knife*   ◆ *Sponge*
◆ *Squeegee*   ◆ *Soft cloth*

1 Gather all your materials together before starting. Wearing goggles for protection, snip the tiles roughly into quarters. Place them in color-graded bowls.

2 Sand the door of the cabinet. Scoring will help secure the tiles to the surface.

3 To make a template of the turtle on page 111, photocopy or trace the design. Enlarge to fit the cabinet door as required.

4 Glue the design to cardboard and cut out.

5 Place the template on the cabinet door and draw around it with a pen.
(See picture at top of next column)

6 With the nippers, cut the copper glass tiles for the outside edge of the turtle into thin rectangles.

7 Spread adhesive/grout onto the back of the tile and place it on the circle line. Continue until the circle is complete.

8 In the same way, fill the turtle shell, working in lines from top to bottom, alternating green and terracotta quarter tiles. Cut individual pieces to fit at the edges.

9 Using the tile nippers cut two small and irregularly shaped copper pieces to make the turtle's eye.

10 Fill in the head, tail, and legs with matte gray-white tiles, clipping and adhering each one as you need it.

11 Next, fill in the turtle background with matte blue tiles.

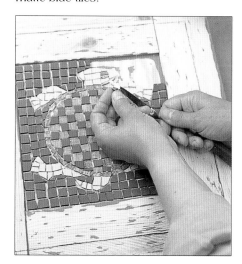

12 For the outside border, fill in the terra-cotta key design. *(See next column)*

13 Add the bold matte blue squares at the corners then complete with copper glass tile centers.

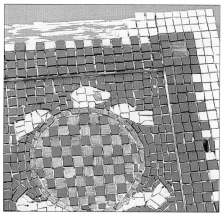

14 Finally, fill in the outside edge with gray-white tiles.

15 Using a palette knife, thoroughly coat the tiled surface with the adhesive/grout mixture, working it in well between the tiles.

16 Use a squeegee to remove most of the excess and to push the grout between the tiles.

17 Use a damp sponge and plenty of water to wipe the surface clean. Dry with a soft cloth.

18 When the grout is completely dry, use a palette knife and the adhesive/grout mixture to neatly fill in the gaps around the outside edge of the mosaic.

19 Let dry for about an hour, then wipe clean with a damp sponge.

20 Paint the cabinet sides, top, and bottom to match the door.

PUTTING IT TOGETHER

metallic-effect cabinet

The exotic-looking metallic finish would lend a striking color accent to any room. With the help of metallic powdered pigments (available at home decorator's and art supply stores), this effect is not difficult to achieve.

98 ◀

MATERIALS

- ◆ *Unfinished cabinet*
- ◆ *Tracing paper and pencil*
- ◆ *Stencil board and ruler*
- ◆ *Craft knife*
- ◆ *Masking tape*
- ◆ *Fine grade sandpaper*
- ◆ *Interior filler (if needed)*
- ◆ *Acrylic primer*
- ◆ *Off-white acrylic paint*
- ◆ *Terracotta acrylic paint*
- ◆ *Acrylic matte medium*
- ◆ *Decorator's sponge*
- ◆ *Selection of powdered metallic pigments or ready-mixed water-based metallic paints*
- ◆ *Metallic car spray paint*
- ◆ *Selection of small brushes*
- ◆ *PVA glue*
- ◆ *Water-based eggshell-finish varnish*
- ◆ *Jars for mixing paints and glazes*

1 Make a tracing with a checkerboard design. Glue the tracing to stencil board. Use a craft knife to cut out the squares.

2 Sand the cabinet and fill in any holes. Allow to dry and sand flat. Mask off any glass panels.

3 Brush on a coat of primer and let dry. Add a coat of off-white acrylic.

4 Mix one part terracotta with one part matte medium and two parts water. Sponge the mixture over the inside and outside of the cabinet. Use a brush to get into tight corners.

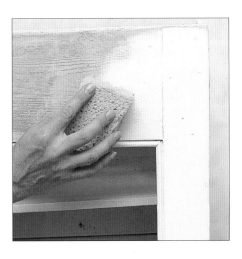

5 Add metallic powder to the PVA glue until it is the consistency of light cream. Add a small amount of water. Using a small brush, transfer the mixture to a decorator's sponge. Using the sponge and PVA mixture, coat the cabinet inside and out. Let dry.

6 Mask the position of the first stripe. Mix a second mixture of a different color metallic powder and PVA glue and sponge on between the first masked lines. Let dry.

7 Remove the tape. Apply a new strip over the painted stripe so the second stripe will abut the first.

8 Place a second piece of masking tape in the position you would like the second stripe to end.

9 Make another metallic mixture and repeat. Continue until the whole cabinet is painted with stripes.

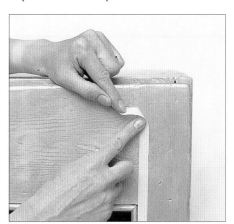

10 Using masking tape, mark a border around the glazed section and paint it in terracotta acrylic paint.

11 Paint a bright gold and PVA mixture onto the decorator's sponge. Using the stencil, sponge on the border. Brush the gold over the beading.

12 Spray paint the inside of the cabinet following the manufacturer's instructions. Let dry.

13 Lightly sand the whole surface, then seal with a water-based eggshell varnish.

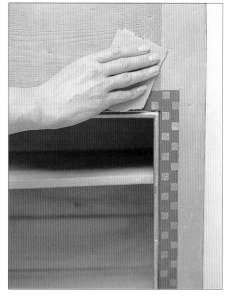

découpage chest

Torn squares, rectangles, and triangles of recycled paper give this chest of drawers a completely new look. A final coat of varnish applied to the finished work lends a translucency to the papers, and provides a protective finish.

MATERIALS
◆ *Chest of drawers*
◆ *Acrylic primer*
◆ *Fine sandpaper*
◆ *Selection of papers such as brown paper, Japanese handmade paper, tissue*
◆ *Steel straight edge*
◆ *Pencil*
◆ *Scissors*
◆ *PVA glue*
◆ *Flat-finish oil-based varnish*
◆ *Pieces of weathered oak for drawer handles*
◆ *Small saw for trimming handles*
◆ *2in/5cm bolts—one for each single handle, and two for the doubles*
◆ *Washers and nuts to fit the bolts*
◆ *Wood glue*
◆ *Drill with bit to fit bolt holes*
◆ *Selection of brushes*
◆ *Pale cream acrylic paint*

1 Sand and prime the drawers.

2 For the decorative panels, measure the width and length of the drawer fronts and draw the dimensions onto your choice of paper.

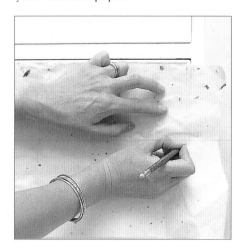

3 Hold a straight edge against the drawn line and tear carefully.

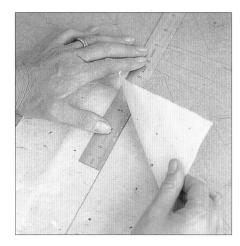

4 Cut paper strips to cover the edges of each drawer.

5 Tear or cut with scissors a variety of shapes and patterns, such as squares, strips, zigzags, and triangles.

6 Position each shape on the drawer fronts. Brush PVA onto the back and front of each shape and apply in position. Brush the drawer front with PVA.

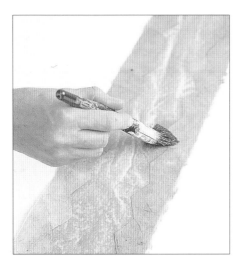

7 In the same way, apply PVA to the strips that will cover the drawer edges and glue into place. Bring the edge piece neatly over the side, adding more paper if needed. Repeat until all the drawers are covered.

8 Use a similar method to cover the top and sides of the chest. Apply one large piece to completely cover the top or side, then apply the decoration.

9 Allow the drawers to dry completely, then brush the whole unit with flat varnish. Allow to dry.

10 Trim the handles to size and sand down. Paint with pale cream acrylic paint thinned with water.

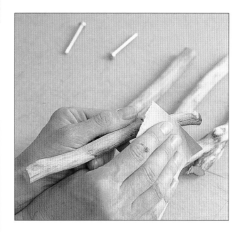

11 Drill ½in/1cm holes into the handles in appropriate places. Align with screw holes on the drawers. Do not drill right through the handles. Apply wood glue to one screw head, then push this into the handle. Place the handle screws into the holes in the drawer front and fix at the back with a washer and nut.

▶ 101

beaded lampshade

❖

Choose a shape over which to make this lampshade. A tall, slim terracotta pot was used for this shade. Try the shape over the base before you begin.

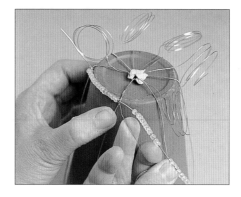

MATERIALS
- ◆ *A shape over which to make the beaded shade*
- ◆ *Medium-grade galvanized garden wire*
- ◆ *Reel of fine florists' wire*
- ◆ *Sticky tack*
- ◆ *Beads*
- ◆ *Jewelry pliers and snippers*
- ◆ *Small lamp carrier*

1 Cut three lengths of galvanized wire long enough to run up one side of the shade, over the top and down the other side, with a little extra at both ends. Space these evenly around the shape to form six struts.

2 Cut three long strands of fine florists' wire, curl the ends, then hold in position with sticky tack on top of the pot.

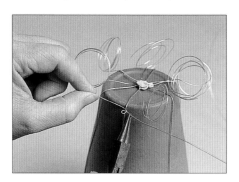

3 Thread the beads of your choice on a long coil of galvanized wire. Do not cut the end of the wire.

4 Using the jewelry pliers, fix the free end of the wire onto a strut at the top of the lampshade.

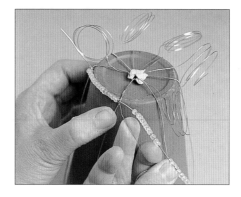

5 Carefully push the beads up along the wire, then bind the beaded wire firmly in place at the next strut with the florists' wire.

6 Continue winding the beaded wire around the form and binding it in place until the shape is complete.

7 At the end, snip off the wire and use the pliers to make a small loop to secure.

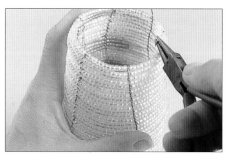

8 Remove the beaded shade from the base. At the top and bottom, neatly fold in the top and bottom struts with pliers.

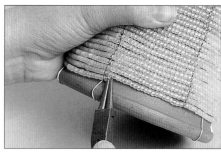

9 Place the lamp carrier into the lampshade and wire into position using the florists' wire.

hammered mirror frame

Roofing flashing is easy to handle, and can be used to create fabulous effects.

MATERIALS
- *Medium-density fiberboard (MDF) 18in/46cm square*
- *Jigsaw or fretsaw*
- *Roofing flashing 6in/15cm wide*
- *Steel rule and craft knife*
- *Water-proofed cloth tape*
- *Ball-headed hammer*
- *Mirrored glass 12in/30cm square*
- *Four mirror corners and screws*
- *Keyhole hanger and screws*

1 Cut out a 10in/25cm square from the MDF to make a 4in/10cm wide frame.

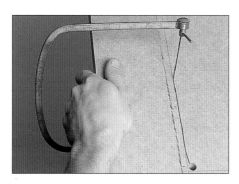

2 Cut four pieces of flashing 18in/46cm long. Measure 1in/2.5cm in from each long edge and draw a line along the length. These are the foldlines.

3 Measure 4in/10cm in from each short end and mark on the foldline.

4 Draw a miter from the marked 4in/10cm point to the corner at the opposite side. Cut along this line. Repeat at the other end. Make four.

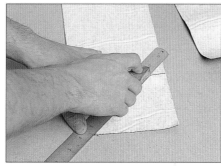

5 Try the pieces against the frame. Peel off the backing and stick each in place.

6 Fold the 1in/2.5cm edges in and stick to the back of the frame.

7 Using the cloth tape, cover the turned-over edges of the flashing.

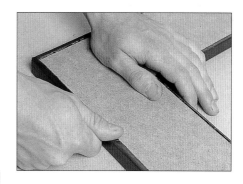

8 Turn the frame to the front. Using a ball-headed hammer cover the whole surface of the flashing with a random pattern of indentations.

9 Screw the mirror glass in place using mirror corners. Pack with cardboard to ensure a snug fit.

10 Screw a key hole hanger to the centre of the back of the frame. Use washers as spacers to bring the hanger level with the back surface of the glass.

painted floorcloth

❖

A simple geometric pattern is easy to paint on a floorcloth. Some suppliers of cotton duck will prime and turn in the edges for you. If you choose to do this process, first wash the floorcloth, then prime it with watered-down acrylic primer. Finally, turn in and stitch a hem.

MATERIALS
- ◆ *Tracing paper and pencil*
- ◆ *Stencil board and craft knife*
- ◆ *Acrylic or latex paints in two values of the same color*
- ◆ *Decorator's sponge*
- ◆ *Large and small paint brushes*
- ◆ *Ruler*
- ◆ *Tape measure*
- ◆ *Flat acrylic varnish*

1 Dilute one part of the lighter paint with two parts water.

2 Apply the diluted paint to the floorcloth with a sponge. Let dry. Apply a second coat with a large paint brush. Let dry.

3 Paint a dark border around the cloth with a small brush.

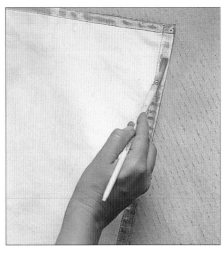

4 Determine the size of the border rectangles and the checker squares. Cut a stencil for each of these.

5 On the floorcloth, lightly draw out squares corresponding to the dimensions of the stencil.

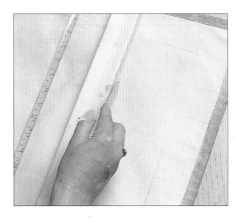

6 Using the stencil and sponge and beginning at one corner, apply the darker color to alternate squares to create a checkerboard design. Continue until all the squares are complete. Repeat with the other color (undiluted).

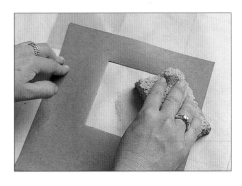

7 Enhance the color of each square by shading with a brush. Start at the edge of each square and work the color in toward the middle. Let dry.

8 Lightly sand the surface of the cloth with fine sandpaper.

9 Finish with flat acrylic varnish.

driftwood bathmat

Pieces of driftwood and leather thong make an unusual textured bathmat.

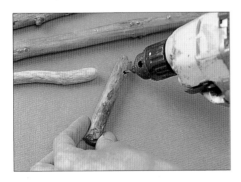

MATERIALS
◆ *Two driftwood pieces 20in/50cm long*
◆ *Eleven small toggle-shaped driftwood pieces*
◆ *30 longer lengths of driftwood*
◆ *Roll of leather thong (available from bead suppliers)*
◆ *Electric drill with small bit*

1 Drill six holes at 3½in/9cm intervals along the length of each 20in/50cm length of driftwood. Drill holes in the smaller pieces at the same intervals.

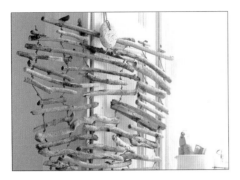

2 Cut five 36in/91cm lengths of leather and tie a knot near the end of each. Thread a small toggle-shaped piece of driftwood onto each one.

3 Tie a second knot at the other side of each toggle and then thread each one into a hole along the length of a 20in/50cm piece of driftwood. Leave one of the central holes free for the hanger. Tie another knot at the other side of the driftwood to secure it.

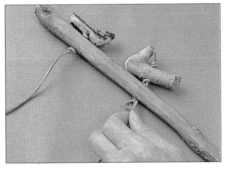

4 Now thread on a piece of short driftwood, tying the thong under that to secure.
(*See picture next column*)

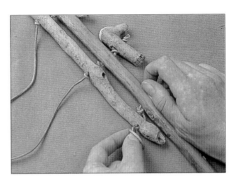

5 Continue tying on pieces of driftwood in a horizontal fashion, and knotting them into position until the mat is 18in/45cm long.

6 Thread on the remaining 20in/50cm piece of driftwood and knot into position. Add a small toggle to finish.

7 To make a hanging loop, thread a loop of leather through the spare hole in the first length of driftwood. Knot it at the bottom of the loop, and then knot the free ends underneath the piece of driftwood. You may wish to finish the hanging with a smooth pebble.

organemdy tablecloth

❖

Glass beads offer an effective and simple way to edge table linen, as they happily withstand the rigors of the washing machine. Slip bead-edged linens into a pillowcase before putting them in the machine to keep them from rattling around and being damaged by the inside of the wash drum.

MATERIALS

♦ 1¼yd/1.2m cotton organdy
♦ Sewing thread in a similar color
♦ Four glass droplets about ½in/15mm long
♦ 45 round glass beads ¼in/5mm long
♦ 96 barrel-shaped glass beads ¼in/5mm long
♦ 45 small round glass beads
♦ Beading needle

1 Iron the fabric to straighten its grain.

2 Turn in and stitch a double hem all around.

3 Using double thread, make a stitch at one corner and thread on a round bead,

a droplet bead, and two barrel beads. Add a tiny glass bead, then pass the thread over the last bead and back through all the other beads.

4 Pull the threads tight, then thread on another barrel bead.

5 Stitch the last bead to the right side of the cloth, at the corner. Finish off at the back. Secure the ends and repeat at the other three corners.

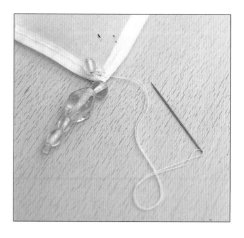

6 Using a similar method and beginning 4½in/11.5cm from one corner, thread on a round bead and a tiny bead. Pass the thread back through the round bead, then sew a barrel bead on at the hem and knot the thread.

7 Continue adding beads along the hem of the cloth.

stunningly simple placemats

❖

These elegant mats are easy to make, and they demonstrate a simple way to make a mitered frame.

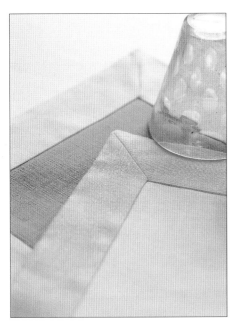

MATERIALS (For six mats)
- *¾yd/0.6m heavy cotton for the main color*
- *½yd/0.5m heavy cotton in a contrasting color*
- *Scissors*
- *Thread*
- *Pins*

1 For each mat, from the main color cut one 18 x 14in/45 x 35cm piece.

2 From the other color, cut two 3 x 14in/7 x 35cm and two 3 x 18in/7 x 45cm strips.

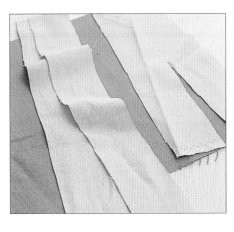

3 Turn down one corner of each end of the strips and fingerpress to mark the miters. Unfold.

4 Place two strips right sides together, then stitch along the crease line. Repeat with the other three strips, stitching each together to make a frame. Trim the miters close to the seams.
(See picture in next column)

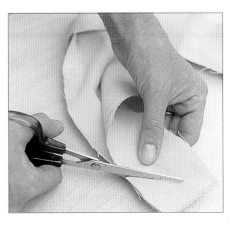

5 Press the miters open.

6 Pin the frame to the main mat piece, right sides together, along the miter seam. Make sure the miter lies flat.

7 Stitch around the outside edge of the mat. Press the seams open and trim.

8 Turn the frame to right side out. Turn in a hem on the inside of the frame. Slipstitch in place.

fishy appliqué tablecloth

❖

Appliqué is a brilliant way to put your own style on any kind of table linen. Adapt this simple design by rearranging these motifs or by choosing your own patterns.

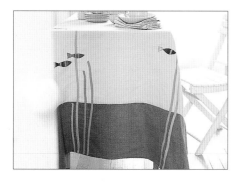

MATERIALS

- 1½ x 1¾yd/1.2 x 1.5m yellow linen
- 1 x 1¾yd/1 x 1.5m aqua linen
- Selection of silks and organzas
- Iron-on fusible webbing
- Matching thread
- Scissors
- Iron
- Embroidery scissors

1 Cut two strips of aqua 12 x 63in/30 x 150cm.

2 Stitch a strip of aqua to each 63in/150cm edge of yellow. Press the seams open.

3 Turn in and stitch a double hem all around the cloth.

4 From scraps, cut reeds 1in/2.5cm wide in varying lengths.

5 Turn in the edges and pin in place. Stitch.

6 Make your own fish templates. Draw one body and tail for each fish, then draw around each template onto the paper backing of the webbing, leaving a large gap around each.

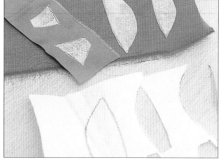

7 Cut out each and place webbing side down on the wrong side of silks and organzas. Fuse together following the manufacturer's instructions.

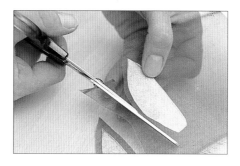

8 Cut out each shape, leaving a ¼in/7mm allowance all around for seams.

9 Turn in the edges of each piece. Clip the corners and curved edges where necessary to create a smooth shape.

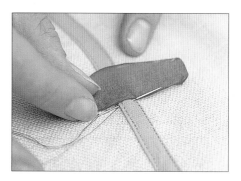

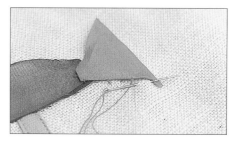

10 Place the fish on the cloth in the desired pattern. Using matching thread, slipstitch into place. Add the tails.

11 To add detail to the body, cut bands of contrasting colors ½in/1cm wide. Turn in the edges and slipstitch in place.

felt placemats

❖

Blanket stitch is a traditional method of decorating and finishing the edges of applied shapes on thick fabrics such as polar fleece and felt.

MATERIALS
For each placemat
- *Tracing paper*
- *Pencil*
- *Scissors*
- *Main felt color 17¾ x 13¾ in/ 45 x 35cm*
- *Scraps of felt in contrasting colors*
- *Contrasting fine wool*
- *Darning needle*

1 Cut the mat to size. Turn in the edges and blanket stitch to secure.
(See picture next column)

2 Make a template of one of the birds on page 110. Use this as a pattern to cut out the shapes from the felt scraps. Position each on the mat and blanket stitch in place.

3 Use satin stitch and stem stitch to create feet and a beak.

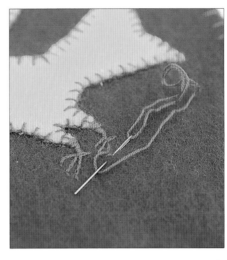

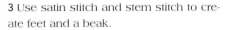

4 Make a large French knot in black for the pupil of the eye and stem stitch around this for the white of the eye.

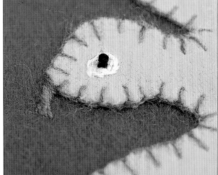

templates

▶ 111

TEMPLATES

index